EASY-TO-DRAW

MONSTERS

by Mattia Cerato & Jannie Ho

PICTURE WINDOW BOOKS
a capstone imprint

MATERIALS

Before you start your amazing drawings, there are a few things you'll need.

PENCIL

COLORED PENCILS

ERASER

MARKERS

RULER

PAPER

SHAPES

Drawing can be easy! If you can draw these simple letters, numbers, and shapes, YOU CAN DRAW anything in this book.

letters

A B C D
T U W

numbers

1 2 3

shapes

lines

Octo-Monster

Clobber

 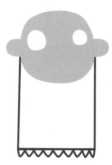  

Gator-Bat

 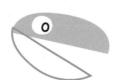  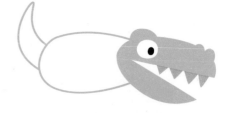

Pinball

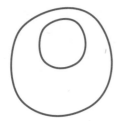   

4

Fearless Boxer

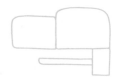  

Use Your Head!

Skater Dino

Batter Up!

Now try this!

7

Bloodshot

Shaggy

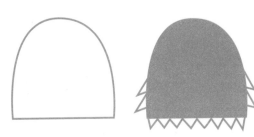

Franken-Fish

Mr. Blob

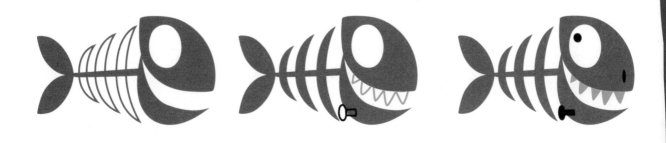

Winged Rocker

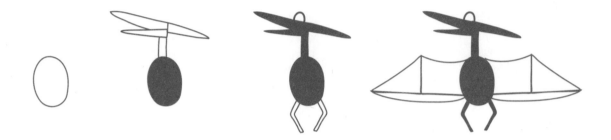

Feathered Drummer

Long-Necked Singer

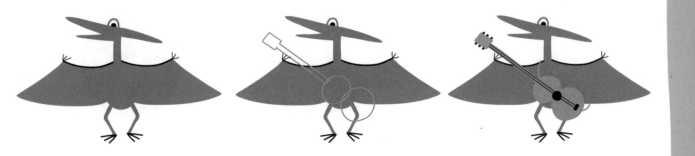

Googly Spider

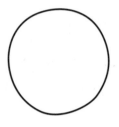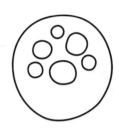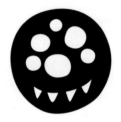

Finger Freak

Boing-O

12

Now try this!

13

Dino Shopper

Snoozing Spike

Flipper

Plated Dino

Papa Monster

Baby Mo

Smelly Foot

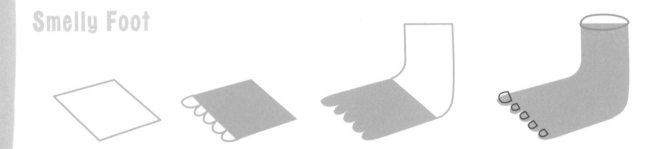

16

Now try this!

17

Out on the Town

Armored Dino

Now try this!

Jack-O'-Lantern

Clawlon

Zeke the Ogre

Time to Hatch!

Weight Lifter

Suspicious Spikes

Feathered Fiend

Nutty Nut

 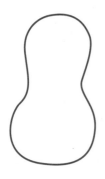 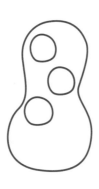  

Funky Chicken

Dancing Dino

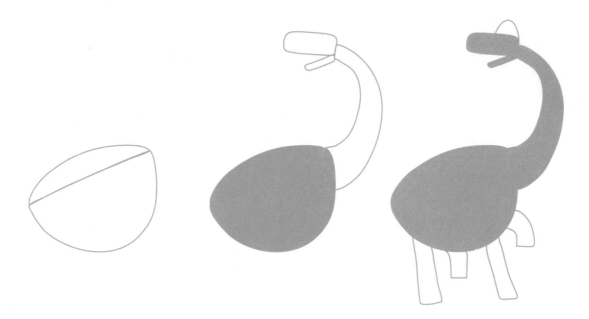

Dribbling Dino

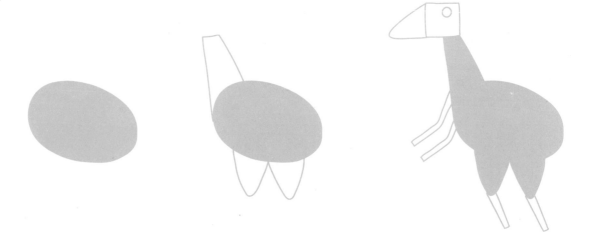

Frankhead

Monstrobot

Crabbo

Venus Fly Trap

Watch Out!

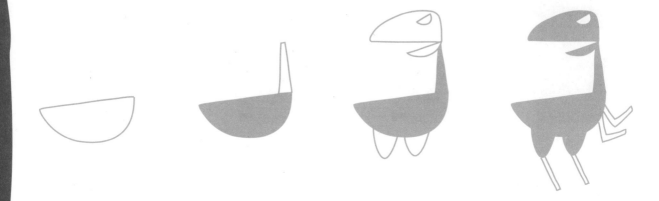

Small But Strong

Dino Racer

Medusa

Freaky Tree

Monkey Mummy

Waving Dino

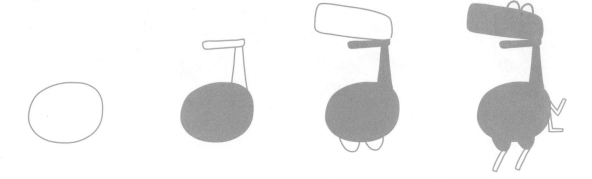

Egg Thief

Woolly Bully

Now that you've drawn all the creepy dinosaurs and monsters,

mash them together
with some crazy props.
What do you get?

A monster
cool party!

Surf Board

Palm Tree

Waves

Swim Fins

Umbrella

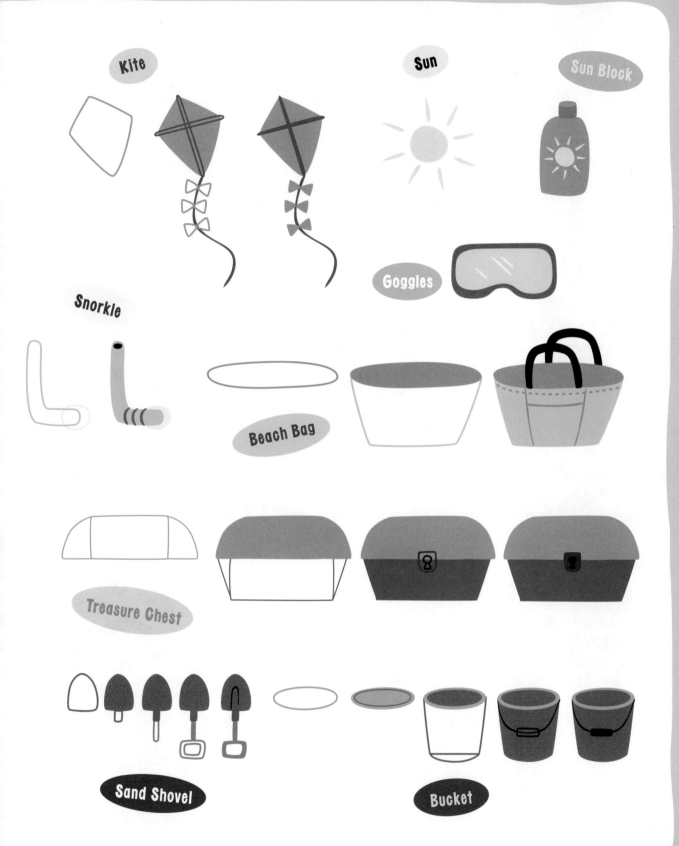

Kite

Sun

Sun Block

Goggles

Snorkle

Beach Bag

Treasure Chest

Sand Shovel

Bucket

PALM TREE

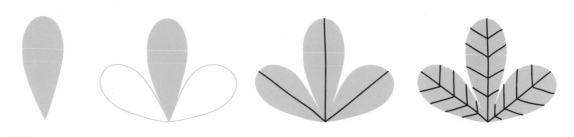

FERN

ROCKS

HOT DOG

HOT DOG IN A BUN

STEAK

MUSTARD AND KETCHUP

VEGGIE LEAF MEAL

COOKOUT TOOL

FORK AND KNIFE

TENT

43

About the Authors

Mattia Cerato was born in Cuneo, a small town surrounded by the beautiful Italian Alps. Besides eating a lot of pasta at the age of 2 or 3, Mattia was introduced to drawing by his father, an artist in his own right. As a result he spent most of his time creating funny images on every surface he could find. When Mattia grew up, he decided to study illustration at the European Institute of Design in Turin, Italy. Within eight months of graduation, he started being represented by the MB Artists of New York City, and ever since then he's illustrated a lot of books. Mattia resides in Turin. When not illustrating, he enjoys playing basketball, traveling around the world, playing his bass guitar, and skiing in the Alps.

Jannie Ho is also known as "Chicken Girl." Born in Hong Kong and raised in Philadelphia, Jannie studied at Parsons The New School for Design in New York City, earning a BFA in illustration. After working as a graphic designer and an art director at places such as Nickelodeon, Scholastic, and *Time Magazine for Kids*, she decided that illustration was her true calling. Jannie now specializes in illustrating for the children's market, with her work appearing in both trade and educational books, magazines, toys, crafts, and digital media. Visit her at www.chickengirldesign.com.

Picture Window Books
151 Good Counsel Drive
P.O. Box 669
Mankato, MN 56002-0669
877-845-8392
www.capstonepub.com

Editor: Shelly Lyons
Designers: Matt Bruning and Tracy Davies
Art Director: Nathan Gassman
Production Specialist: Sarah Bennett
The illustrations in this book were created digitally.

Library of Congress Cataloging-in-Publication Data
Cataloging-in-publication information is on file with the Library of Congress.
ISBN 978-1-4048-6761-1

Printed in Shenzhen, Guangdong, China.
112010
006015